INSIDE STORIES

*With special thanks to
Deborah Bolton for her
patience typing the manuscript.*

*Liza Davies is the founder and director
of Arts Counselling Trust (ACT), a
registered charity which provides
creative therapy for prisoners in
custody and on their release.*

INSIDE STORIES

EDITED BY

LIZA DAVIES

The Bible Reading Fellowship

Text copyright Liza Davies © 1994

The author asserts the moral right to be identified as the author of this work

Published by
The Bible Reading Fellowship
Sandy Lane West,
Oxford, England
ISBN 0 7459 2987 7
Albatross Books Pty Ltd
PO Box 320, Sutherland,
NSW 2232, Australia
ISBN 0 7324 0912 8

First edition 1994
10 9 8 7 6 5 4 3 2 1 0

All rights reserved

Acknowledgments

Scripture quoted from the **Good News Bible**, published by The Bible Societies/HarperCollins Publishers Ltd., UK, © American Bible Society, 1966, 1971, 1976, 1992

'Woodcut' cross by Colin Riches
Photographs by Michael Inns
Illustrations by Richard Pavell

A catalogue record for this book is available from the British Library

Printed and bound in Great Britain by Cox & Wyman Ltd, Reading

Contents

Foreword	6
Introduction	7
When I feel alone	9
Is God really there?	16
When no one understands	23
Listening to God	27
When I'm in despair	39
The healing love of God	43
Knock back!	47
God's promise to me	49
Forgiveness	55
New life	65
Unconditional love	76
When I can't go on	79
Come Holy Spirit	82
No way out	84
God has a plan for my life	86
The still small voice	92
The peace of God	95

Foreword

Stories have an endless fascination and most of us enjoy both hearing and telling them. Think of the way that 'Coronation Street' or 'Neighbours' continues to attract enormous numbers of viewers. Think, too, of the way in which we are drawn into the story, perhaps identifying with a particular character, and certainly wanting to know what happens next, or how a particular situation will end.

All this illustrates the two great characteristics of stories. The first is that they are timeless, and the second is that they draw us into their action. We become caught up in the events themselves, and before we know it, we are 'hooked'.

The Bible too is full of stories—indeed it's been called 'the greatest story ever told'. Certainly it is the longest and most consistent record we have of God's dealings with mankind, and with the world he has made. The way to approach it is the way we approach other stories, with openness and a willingness to be involved ourselves, allowing its stories to speak to us. Most of us, however, need help, because the Bible can appear both daunting and confusing. That is why this book is so useful, for it helps us lay our story alongside that of Scripture, and allows the one to illuminate the other.

+ *Robert Lincoln*
Bishop to prisons

Introduction

William Temple, former Archbishop of Canterbury, wrote, 'The prisoner is never only a criminal and nothing else.'

During my work assisting the Chaplaincy team at HMP Wandsworth I have met with and listened to some remarkably gifted men who, by looking at their life story and personal imprisonment, have been challenged and entered into a personal relationship with God.

Psalm 31 promises that a loving, creator God is our refuge and that he will rescue us from our bondage and affliction. Prison is not just a building. It can be our own life experience or pattern.

By sharing these stories and contributions by men and women who work with prisoners and those who are, or have been, in custody I hope this book may, in some way give you insight into your own situation. Whoever and wherever you are.

But my trust is in you, O Lord;
you are my God.
I am always in your care;
save me from my enemies,
from those who persecute me.
Look on your servant with kindness;
save me in your constant love.

Psalm 31:14–16

When I feel alone

A prison is a place full of people, yet like many other busy or crowded places we can be overcome by an overwhelming sense of aloneness. This may be a feeling which comes and goes, or it may be present with us each day. A question I'm often asked by people (not just in prison) who feel alone is, 'Is there really a God?' 'If there is, why has he abandoned me?' The Scripture promises that there is nowhere we can hide from God and that he is always present with us. This contribution from The Right Revd Philip Goodrich, Bishop of Worcester, explores the theme of feeling alone in prison.

Many a time when I have been conducting a Confirmation in prison I have said, 'You, my brothers (or sisters), you alone can show us what it is to be a Christian in prison.' I might have added, 'One thing, however, that you share with us is the certainty that you will not always get it right. There will be times of failure, times when you feel desperately compromised and terribly in need of forgiveness and restoration.'

One of the things which must afflict those in prison is a sense of being alone, cut off from God. It can bring a sense that our faith was a mistaken fantasy in the first place. We might as

well scrap it all and as for trust in God and his goodness, we might as well forget it. There is nothing in it and there is no one there.

Well, these are feelings which can overtake anyone whether 'inside' or out. At times like this we need awareness of the universal Church. The whole point about membership of the Church is that we build each other up in faith. Your insight compensates for my lack. There may be something in my experience that can assist you. Anyway, faith in the living God is something which the universal Church holds corporately. When I feel most alone and isolated, I remind myself of all those other people in a hundred different places who are believing and praying and living the faith with me and for me and on my behalf—'*We* believe in one God.'

There is also that verse in the Epistle to the Hebrews, 'He [Jesus Christ] lives for ever to plead with God for them'—that is, us, wherever we may be and whatever the time may be. We may be suffering, we may be sleepless, we may have our minds full of strange and frightening thoughts. Remember, at such a time, 'He lives for ever to plead with God for us.' He did not come to earth to share our lot for nothing. He came in order that for ever he might bear us on his heart before the living God, the God of infinite compassion.

There is also the traditional teaching held by believers at all times and part of the faith of the centuries, namely that God is everywhere present. Psalm 139 should be read over and over again:

> *Where could I go to escape from you?*
> *Where could I get away from your presence?*
> *If I went up to heaven, you would be there;*
> *if I lay down in the world of the dead,*
> *you would be there.*
> *If I flew away beyond the east*
> *or lived in the farthest place in the west,*
> *you would be there to lead me,*
> *you would be there to help me.*

It's a conviction expressed in the well-known chorus, 'He's got the whole world in his hands'.

Even in the darkness God is present:

> *… but even darkness is not dark for you,*
> *and the night is as bright as the day.*
> *Darkness and light are the same to you.*

Of course we can say that with our heads but our hearts may feel far from it. Then there is nothing for it but to sweat it out and to go on going on.

Finally, the sense of God's absence is strangely an indication of his presence. Furthermore, we should not be afraid to talk with God, argue with him, complain to him, tell him just how we feel. Out of this may come a robust faith, a faith in tune with the great words of Isaiah, 'Surely he has borne our griefs and carried our sorrows.' For as well as being strong and life-affirming, Jesus Christ, the magnet who still draws thousands to become his disciples, was also 'a man of sorrows and acquainted with grief'. He shares our pains, our sense of isolation and desolation, in order to share with us his victory over them.

*Lord, you have examined me and you know me.
You know everything I do;
from far away you understand all my thoughts.
You see me, whether I am working or resting;
you know all my actions.
Even before I speak,
you already know what I will say.
You are all round me on every side;
you protect me with your power.
Your knowledge of me is too deep;
it is beyond my understanding.*

*Where could I go to escape from you?
Where could I get away from your presence?
If I went up to heaven, you would be there;
if I lay down in the world of the dead,
you would be there.
If I flew away beyond the east
or lived in the farthest place in the west,
you would be there to lead me,
you would be there to help me.
I could ask the darkness to hide me
or the light round me to turn into night,
but even darkness is not dark for you,
and the night is as bright as the day.
Darkness and light are the same to you.*

*You created every part of me;
you put me together in my mother's womb.
I praise you because you are to be feared;*

all you do is strange and wonderful.
I know it with all my heart.
When my bones were being formed,
carefully put together in my mother's womb,
when I was growing there in secret,
you knew that I was there—
you saw me before I was born.
The days allotted to me
had all been recorded in your book,
before any of them ever began.
O God, how difficult I find your thoughts;
how many of them there are!
If I counted them, they would be
more than the grains of sand.
When I awake, I am still with you.

O God, how I wish you would kill the wicked!
How I wish violent people would leave me alone!
They say wicked things about you;
they speak evil things against your name.
O Lord, how I hate those who hate you!
How I despise those who rebel against you!
I hate them with a total hatred;
I regard them as my enemies.

Examine me, O God, and know my mind;
test me, and discover my thoughts.
Find out if there is any evil in me
and guide me in the everlasting way.

Psalm 139

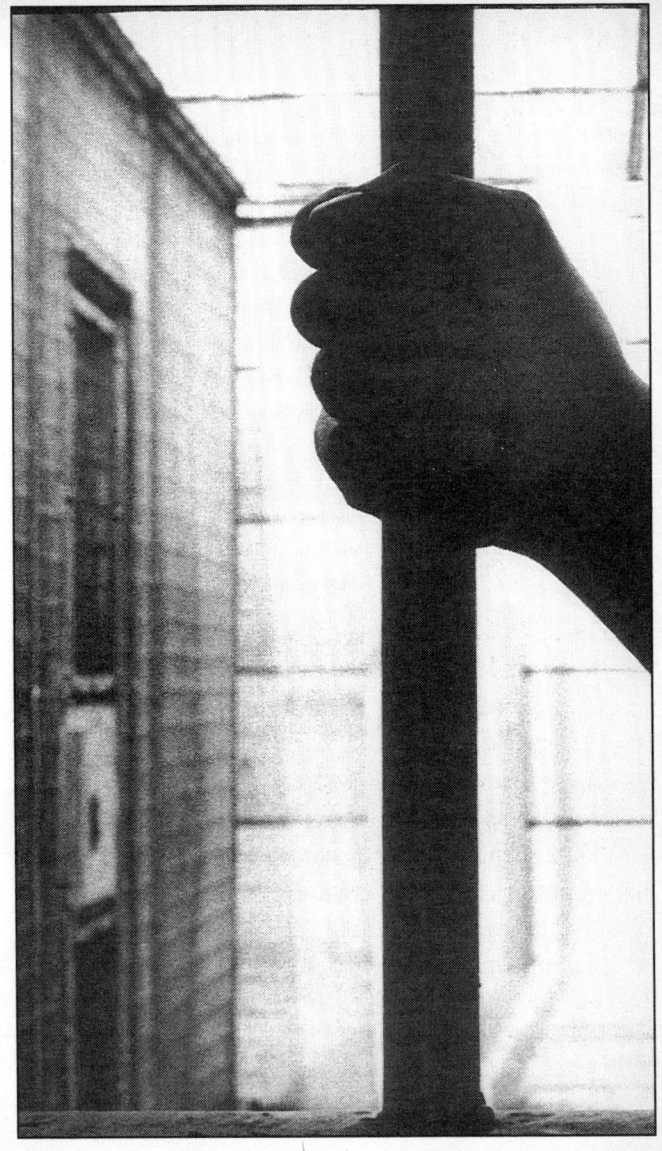

Is God really there?

When we turn away from God's perfect plan for us we fall into a condition Christians know as sin. This condition is like a sickness which eventually eats the whole body and so perhaps the question isn't, 'Is God really there?' but rather, 'Where is God in all this mess?'

For David, whom I met at Lincoln Prison, the reality of God came at a point when it seemed as if life held no future for him.

David's story

I'm out on 25 April 1994 then I don't know what I'm going to do. Since I've been in prison divorce papers have come through and my wife doesn't want anything to do with me. It hurts but I suppose I will get over it. This is my first time in prison. My parents split up when I was eleven. There was seven of us. Eventually my mum got married again to an Irishman. He and I did not get on one bit. When I was fourteen he put his hands up to my mum and I picked up a cast iron handle. I hit him across the shoulder blades then I went upstairs, packed some bags and left. I went around the country; I slept in dykes and bus shelters. I'd tried to protect my mum but I'd had enough.

I came into prison through a domestic fight with my stepdaughter and my wife also got hurt. It was like a repeat of what had happened when I was a child. Basically I had a rough life.

When I first came into prison I had a job in the tailor's shop and then I was asked if I wanted to be chaplain's orderly. I believe this is when I found my faith in God. I sat in the cell reading through the Bible. I was thinking about all the problems that I have and felt someone on the side of the bed, like someone sat beside me. I felt the bed move and I just felt as though everything had been drained from me. I burst out crying with relief.

My cell mate woke up and said, 'What is the problem?' I said, 'Nothing.' It was the first time I'd had an encounter with God. I used to go to church once a month on the outside but I'd never had these feelings.

I feel better in myself: I can get on with my life. Most nights when I go to bed I pray and I feel more relaxed, at ease. Some nights I sit up reading the Bible, say a few prayers, and think about when I first came in. I couldn't sleep and I went four or five days without sleep. Now I can sleep at ease.

I find going to the chapel very helpful. I get others laughing as I come out but that doesn't hurt me—it's up to them.

Through David's call God made himself available. Some prisoners have said to me that they have called on God but he hasn't heard them. God doesn't always appear to us in miraculous visions or send flashes of light—sometimes he sends along a person, a representative who can listen to us or perhaps offer practical help.

Talking with the Chaplain of a Young Offenders' Institution, I asked him the secret of his obvious success with the lads in the establishment. 'Being there, and being available' was his reply. That is exactly what Christians believe God has done through Jesus Christ. He has come to us and made himself available.

> **For God loved the world so much that he gave his only Son, so that everyone who believes in him may not die but have eternal life.**

John 3:16

+ *Robert Lincoln*

Philip Meaden is Chaplain at Wandsworth Prison in London. He has worked with prisoners for more than seventeen years.

Prisoners in English prisons are the consequences of a society which has forgotten its Christian roots. So often our society is motivated by the pursuit of wealth in all its many forms. In our society it is widely believed that possessions are what give value and dignity to a person. One of the few advantages of being in prison is that people have time to reflect and to think about spiritual riches.

I have chosen three examples to illustrate the profound change that can take place in a prisoner's life. I do not wish to be misunderstood, for there is a type of 'prison religion' where an inmate can and does make a profession of faith in order to avoid responsibility or to seek to please. This type of religion lasts only as long as the prison sentence. It is unfortunate that this false religion so often discredits Christian ministry to prisoners.

First I should like to tell of a young police officer who had received a four-year sentence for assault. During the time that I knew him, he undertook an honest examination of his life, which before entry into prison had been one of dishonesty and drunkenness. The offence which had resulted in his sentence was only the last in a series of crimes. In this person I observed a genuine change, for he demonstrated to my satisfaction and to many others', that he had learned from his life before prison. One can but imagine the difficulties which he experienced, being a former policeman and endeavouring to live a changed life. His fortitude and self-discipline in the face of so much cynicism, was both astonishing and admirable.

A second example is of a young man who was about eighteen years old and was serving a life sentence. He had stabbed to death a member of a rival gang after a football match. As with my previous example, he underwent a complete change as a result of that action. While in prison he worked in the library and I was amongst others who experienced his strong and quiet faith. I knew him for a period of six years and saw him almost every day, and never heard him speak ill or insult anyone. He succeeded in living in prison and was a continuing witness to his faith despite the corrupting influence of the institution.

My last example is of a prisoner who has influenced me in the most profound way. This was a man who had stabbed and killed a Black man. This inmate was a skinhead and a member of an extreme right-wing party. He was a born leader and led a violent and vicious gang who for recreation beat up Black and Asian people. When I knew him, he was nineteen years old and had already changed dramatically.

I have known few men, even few priests, with a faith so deep and mature as his. He still had the same leadership qualities, and by his behaviour and his life of prayer he was one of the most astonishing examples of what the Holy Spirit can do in anyone's life. This young man knew the Scriptures very well and I must admit that instead of me ministering to him, it was often he who ministered to me.

I remember one occasion when he asked me to obtain a book of the writings of Julian of Norwich. Within a few weeks he had absorbed and made this important Christian work his own. At times when I felt down or unhappy, a visit to his cell and being in his company for a few minutes made me feel immensely better.

He had a talent for speaking about the Christian faith through the Scriptures and through Christian spiritual writings, especially that which I have mentioned, which was simple and direct and devoid of any element of preaching. At one point when I was doubting my ministry both as a priest and Chaplain, he gave me the courage and strength to go on.

I have known several other examples of men like these during my seventeen years of ministry. I continue in the work, not only because I can bring the comfort of the gospel but because I find myself in the company of those who bring me comfort. For me, prison chaplaincy is the most Christian of callings.

> *The Lord said to me, 'I chose you before I gave you life, and before you were born I selected you to be a prophet to the nations.'*
>
> *I answered, 'Sovereign Lord, I don't know how to speak; I am too young.'*
>
> *But the Lord said to me, 'Do not say that you are too young, but go to the people I send you to, and tell them everything I command you to say.'*
>
> Jeremiah 1:4–7

When no one understands

How many times in our lives does it seem that, whatever we say to our friends, loved ones or colleagues, we are misunderstood and what we say or do is used against us? We can become outcasts. Many of the people whom Jesus met were misunderstood and rejected by the community where they lived.

In the story of the woman at the well, Jesus meets a Samaritan woman. Jesus knew all about her, how she lived and who she had relationships with. Unlike the disciples and the people of the village, who despised her, Jesus reached out to her. He understood this woman and why she had lived as she had. He knew all she had done, yet he did not reject her. He knew her heart. God reaches out to you and to me in friendship, just as he reached out to the Samaritan woman.

Consider the story and try to imagine yourself there—perhaps you know what it feels like to be completely rejected as she was. The promise is that God does understand you. Maybe there are things about your life that you long to change. God knows you can't do them alone. Just as Jesus reached out to this woman, if you trust in him he can also meet with you.

Jesus talks with a Samaritan woman

The Pharisees heard that Jesus was winning and baptizing more disciples than John. (Actually, Jesus himself did not baptize anyone; only his disciples did.) So when Jesus heard what was being said, he left Judea and went back to Galilee; on his way there he had to go through Samaria.

In Samaria he came to a town named Sychar, which was not far from the field that Jacob had given to his son Joseph. Jacob's well was there, and Jesus, tired out by the journey, sat down by the well. It was about noon.

A Samaritan woman came to draw some water, and Jesus said to her, 'Give me a drink of water.' (His disciples had gone into town to buy food.)

The woman answered, 'You are a Jew, and I am a Samaritan—so how can you ask me for a drink?' (Jews will not use the same cups and bowls that Samaritans use.)

Jesus answered, 'If only you knew what God gives and who it is that is asking you for a drink, you would ask him, and he would give you life-giving water.'

'Sir,' the woman said, 'you haven't got a bucket, and the well is deep. Where would you get that life-giving water? It was our ancestor Jacob who gave us this well; he and his sons and his flocks all drank from it. You don't claim to be greater than Jacob, do you?'

Jesus answered, 'All those who drink this water will be thirsty again, but whoever drinks the water *that I will give him will never be thirsty again. The water that I will give him will become in him a spring which will provide him with life-giving water and give him eternal life.'*

'Sir,' the woman said, 'give me that water! Then I will never be thirsty again, nor will I have to come here to draw water.'

'Go and call your husband,' Jesus told her, 'and come back.'

'I haven't got a husband,' she answered. Jesus replied, 'You are right when you say you haven't got a husband. You have been married to five men, and the man you live with now is not really your husband. You have told me the truth.'

'I see you are a prophet, sir,' the woman said. 'My Samaritan ancestors worshipped God on this mountain, but you Jews say that Jerusalem is the place where we should worship God.'

Jesus said to her, 'Believe me, woman, the time will come when people will not worship the Father either on this mountain or in Jerusalem. You Samaritans do not really know whom you worship; but we Jews know whom we worship, because it is from the Jews that salvation comes. But the time is coming and is already here, when by the power of God's Spirit people will worship the Father as he really is, offering him the true worship that he wants. God is Spirit, and only by the power of his Spirit can people worship him as he really is.'

The woman said to him, 'I know that the Messiah will come, and when he comes, he will tell us everything.'

Jesus answered, 'I am he, I who am talking with you.'

Listening to God

*'Don't be stupid like a horse or a mule,
which must be controlled with a bit and bridle
to make it submit.'*

*The wicked will have to suffer,
but those who trust in the Lord
are protected by his constant love.*

Psalm 32:9–10

Have you ever noticed that someone may ask you for help, or advice, and then fail to take any notice or listen to what you have to say? Our relationship with God can be just like that too. We call to him for help but then fail to give him space in which to respond or don't like the response we get. In Ralph's story the one thing which sustained him throughout the chaos of travelling to his mother's funeral was the inner peace which came from listening to God. Ralph put the day completely in the Lord's hands and yet, even when it all seemed to be going wrong, this sense of peace remained with him.

Ralph's story—my day out

The Chaplain had just left my cell after informing me of the death of my mother. I was now head of the family, but a black sheep. Seeking guidance, I prayed about it. I am serving a two-and-a-half-year sentence and only four months had passed by. My sister had asked if I could be taken to her home, prior to the cortège leaving her house, after a short service in which I would actively participate. We thought this would overcome my reluctance to appear at the funeral handcuffed to a prison officer (my immediate family knew of my circumstances but not my mother's personal friends).

The Governor's decision was different. I would be flown to Aberdeen, attend the service at the appointed place, and return immediately. But it did not work like that. On the morning of the funeral I was up, washed, dressed and said my prayers by half past six. I felt quite at peace with myself and the world as I waited in my cell to be collected.

Mr A and Miss J were to be my escorting officers for the day. I changed from my prison gear into my own clothes in reception. The officers assigned to guard me were also in 'mufti' and Mr A said I would be able to borrow his black tie for the service. We left the prison in the comfort of a hired car.

Miss J and Mr A exchanged pleasantries with the driver and I looked out of my window at the passing scene. The funeral service was due at eleven o'clock and the crematorium was fifteen miles from Aberdeen Airport. I thought the timing was a bit fine, but we had no luggage and maybe we had special clearance for our flight.

We were then pulled up on the hard shoulder of the motorway by a police car. Continuing our journey, we had two more miles to go and had lost fifteen minutes. Things were a bit tighter now. With a few minutes to spare we reached the information desk at the north terminal. Turning from the desk, Miss J looked at us with a glum face. 'We should be at the south terminal.'

We made for the airport police station and parked outside. I still retained my inner peace. It was as though I was in a state of remoteness, not part of what was happening around me. Wandsworth was telephoned and gave instructions: 'Get him to Aberdeen, take off time is 10:18.'

Our seat allocation was made quite quickly. Off we dashed to Gate 52 and arrived breathless at an empty departure gate five minutes late. We found out it should have been Gate 6—a considerable distance away—and more than one head turned to watch us run past. Eventually we reached an almost deserted departure lounge and I could see the plane pulling out from its bay.

We walked dejectedly back to the car and made our way to the police station. We waited patiently fully expecting to be recalled, but, no, to our great surprise, the order was 'get that man to Aberdeen!!'. It was nearly eleven o'clock, the time of the funeral service. I bowed my head in prayer and prayed for all my family, relatives and mother's friends. I thanked the Lord for my mother's life and I prayed for his continued protection. I then sang two of my mother's favourite hymns and enjoyed my solitary service. I was then told some startling news. I was to be taken to my sister's home direct from Aberdeen Airport to enable me to be with my kinsfolk and share in a short family service, just as we had asked for in our original request to the Governor.

No man could have planned the preceding events. Providence had prevailed. I thanked God as I was led handcuffed to the waiting plane. We were first to board the lunchtime flight. Before I took my window seat at the rear of the place, Mr A unlocked and removed my restraint.

Sitting looking out of the small window at the sunlit apron I felt completely at peace with the world. I felt free. Free for the first time since I was arrested.

My wife, son, and sister stood in the driveway of her bungalow as we drove in. Their smiles of welcome made everything so worthwhile even though I was wearing handcuffs. Soon we were embracing each other—shaking hands with my cousins, nephews and nieces with my left hand was no problem.

After the warm welcome, we shared a simple service in dedication to my mother and gave thanks to the Lord for my being there with them. We had a very enjoyable two hours together, but all too soon the time came to leave. No tears, no complaints, just a lot of love. Farewells were made, hugs, kisses, handshakes and waving of arms. As we travelled to Dyce (Aberdeen Airport) I knew instinctively I had to prepare myself for what was waiting for me at the end of my journey.

At Dyce I was shown into a cell, but not 'banged up'. My inner peace prevailed and I 'wondered' at the timing of the day's events. Parts of Scripture flittered into my head.

'My ways are not your ways...' 'My timing is not yours...' '...his wonders to perform.'

Time to move again. Once more padlocked at the wrist we walked to the aeroplane.

Listening to God is also about giving him room to be with us at all times and in all situations. Consider God as your life's walking companion. Perhaps one of the best known Psalms in the Bible is Psalm 23 which describes God's presence with us wherever we are, daily leading us closer to him even to the end of our lives when we shall see God face to face.

The Lord is my shepherd;
I have everything I need.
He lets me rest in fields of green grass
and leads me to quiet pools of fresh water.
He gives me new strength.
He guides me in the right paths,
as he has promised.
Even if I go through the deepest darkness,
I will not be afraid, Lord,
for you are with me.
Your shepherd's rod and staff protect me.

You prepare a banquet for me,
where all my enemies can see me;
you welcome me as an honoured guest
and fill my cup to the brim.
I know that your goodness and love
will be with me all my life;
and your house will be my home
as long as I live.

Psalm 23

I met Brian not long after he had started his second sentence. This is his story and describes how, through listening, God has brought him to a new understanding of himself.

Brian's story

I've been in Wandsworth for eight months and before that I spent three and a half months on remand in Brixton. The first time I served six months of a twelve-month sentence. I am now serving five years. The first 24 hours of my first prison sentence were unlike anything I'd ever experienced before. It just seemed like a dream. One minute I was standing in the court hugging my wife and the next thing I was in a bus chained to other people. One hour later I was in a shower where all vestiges of my hitherto seeming independence were taken away from me and, suddenly, the door was slammed.

I found the biggest thing to get used to was moving from an environment where I was operating two and sometimes three phones at once to suddenly find that there were no phones. Just really having to wind down was one of the most difficult parts of the early days of my sentence.

One of my great difficulties was that I found it hard to share my burdens with my wife and right up to the day when I was imprisoned there was much of my story which I had not been able to confide in her. The burdens were just so great I felt that I didn't want her to know about them and when she found the mass of untold stories that I'd left behind when I went to prison the first time it devastated her.

My first morning in prison, on my first sentence, was

quite revealing. I was sentenced on Friday and on Saturday morning I was sitting with the Chaplain, which was just a routine visit for new inmates coming in each day. He asked me if I would like to go to the service on Sunday and without any sort of a thought I said yes. My daughter had been christened in our local church and prior to that the local vicar had come along to my wife and myself and we had sat and discussed various aspects of belief. We weren't regular churchgoers.

On my second day in prison it seemed as though I'd reached the very lowest ebb of my life. Things were going on around which I didn't understand, things had happened to me which made me feel, like most people do when they come to prison, what on earth am I doing here? I felt that I needed to make an appeal to someone for a bit of guidance and it was more through hope rather than conviction or faith that I continued to go to church. It made me feel good when I came out of the service. It made me feel as though at last here was the help that perhaps I should have been appealing for when I was outside prison, which had got me into my difficulties.

I was then transferred to an open prison and I came into contact with a lady who was on the board of visitors, who was also the choirmistress of the prison. I thought there was some driving force in this lady's life which I wanted, too. I didn't know what it was, but she had got something special. From that my faith simply developed to the extent that I became very closely attached to the Chaplaincy. Yet at the back of my mind I did not really know what was going to happen when I was released.

The morning I was due to leave the chaplain came to me and said 'have faith in God'. I took him at his word. I had full intentions of continuing the journey that I'd started, so to speak, a journey of faith. I returned to my local community and joined a Bible study class.

When I went out I found that life was even more difficult and I didn't feel that my first sentence had achieved anything or solved any of my problems. It had just delayed things for six months. I continued to have faith but somehow the ends were not tying up. I went out determined to try and rebuild a life in the way that I wanted to rebuild it and I wanted to prove everyone wrong, but I couldn't get out of these problems that I had got into by my own foolishness. I had debts in the region of a quarter of a million pounds. I created more pressure for myself and within five months I was back inside facing a much more serious charge and was sentenced to five years. It was only at that time that I realized that the mistake I had made was that I had not changed myself through my faith, that changes have to be made from within, and I set about looking at what changes needed to be made to my life.

My first reaction to my wife wanting to come and visit me was to ask her not to do so. I'd received much support from her and my family the first time I was in prison and I felt that I'd just kicked them in the teeth. I asked her to go away, with my three-year-old daughter, to forget about me and to get on with their lives. She said that she was not going to abandon me, irrespective of whatever I'd done. Her strength of character never fails to surprise me. I asked her to keep her correspondence down to a minimum; I chose not to write any letters the whole three and a half months that I was on remand

and not to see any of my family. For quite different reasons I didn't want to see my young daughter. I didn't want to make my wife's life any more difficult by my daughter being more confused, and at the time this seemed to me to be the right decision.

I think my biggest change is the fact that I would like to see myself now as a person who can look at matters which I've been involved in objectively, rather than taking the attitude which we see all too often in prison: 'Well, that's my view and I don't care what you think and that's the way it's going to be,' without any attempt to show compromise. I was always a short-tempered person and whether that was brought on by the kind of stress I was under I'm not entirely sure. I've tried to curb that temper: instead of confronting a situation, I'd sooner walk away from it, though. I always felt as though I had to get the last word in. I don't feel as though I woke up one morning and suddenly had this urge no longer to argue with anyone: it was simply a question of searching deep down into my soul. I'd gone into the depths and admitted things to myself which I would never have admitted to before all the façade had been taken away.

Suddenly you find yourself at the very base level of human existence. From that moment on no matter what kind of brickbats people throw at you it's a rebuilding process, that moves on. Somehow you get the courage, or inspiration, that you would never have otherwise had, and it's only by stripping down these layers that you find out what your strengths really are. I don't know how fragile the building blocks that I'm building on are. At the moment I'm in a cocooned environment—prison. It's very difficult to relate what goes on in here to what goes on in the real world. You can theorize while you're in here—my life's going to go this way or that way—but once you get outside you find that it's like walking against the rush hour. You've got masses of people walking at you from different directions and your attention on things that you are trying to focus on in life suddenly becomes deflected.

It would be quite easy for me to say that my efforts to rehabilitate myself will be a success but I honestly don't know if that will be the case. What I can do is look for guidance; and as the months pass by there are occasions where I find that I'm drifting into a kind of spiritual neutrality where I'm looking more towards how I'm going to look after myself and my family when I get out. What I should be doing is looking for inspiration from within through my faith to give me the answers, because the answers that I've been given so far just instinctively seem to be the right answers.

When I'm in despair

Despair can often turn into self-pity. In turn we cut ourselves off from friends, family and, most often, those who are closest and love us most. For Jon his despair came the through lack of being able to choose what was happening to him—yet he did have some choices about what to do with his time instead of sitting alone in a cell. In my own life I have often been tempted to 'opt out': to give in to low self-esteem and choose not to see any alternatives. Making the choice is the hardest thing, but once made it may open doors of light into what appears an impossible problem.

Jon's story—my battle with despair

Coming into prison for the first time was a very daunting experience. I felt really scared and I was filled with despair. I didn't know who to turn to, what to expect and I was confused about my future. For the first time in my life I had no control over what was happening to me.

I had spent most of my life in the military and so I saw the prison as an extension of that régime and I adapted to it accordingly. However, I couldn't cope with the continuous 'bang up' and so I looked for ways to escape from the confines of my prison cell. The monotony of the workshops didn't interest me and there was a waiting list for education so I had to find other avenues. I found the Church.

I have never been interested in or had much to do with religion. I was ordered to go to church at Christmas, Remembrance Sunday and at Easter but now, here in prison, I was attending the Sunday services regularly. It gave me an opportunity to spend an hour out of my cell. I soon discovered that the Chaplaincy ran Bible classes three times a week and so I applied to attend these as another means of 'escape' from my cell and a chance to mix with other inmates.

The classes gave me an opportunity to play 'devil's advocate'—which was sheer arrogance and ignorance on my part—and there were some quite lively debates. But slowly, a bit like a flower beginning to bloom, I began to learn. I learned a lot from these classes, not just the Scriptures but about people and, more importantly, I learned about myself.

One day I asked myself one very important question: 'Do I now attend Bible classes to escape my cell or do I now attend because I enjoy them?' The biggest test came when association was introduced as it clashed with the Bible classes and I found myself choosing to go to the classes.

Over the months I have changed my life and my way of thinking. I have become tolerant, friendly, caring and open to other people's views and opinions. Sure, I still have many faults but I am working on them.

What do I get out of these classes? I receive a peace of mind and contentment in the knowledge that I am among friends all with a common goal. A rare trait in prison.

I still get depressed—who doesn't—but when I do I turn to a favourite passage of Scripture which eases my mind and takes away despair.

> *The Lord is a refuge for the oppressed,*
> *a place of safety in times of trouble.*
> *Those who know you, Lord, will trust you;*
> *you do not abandon anyone who comes to you.*

Psalm 9:9–10

The story in Luke's Gospel about a woman bleeding for twelve years demonstrates that choice is an act of faith. A belief that we do not have to stay with our despair.

A dead girl and a sick woman

As Jesus went along, the people were crowding him from every side. Among them was a woman who had suffered from severe bleeding for twelve years; she had spent all she had on doctors, but no one had been able to cure her. She came up in the crowd behind Jesus and touched the edge of his cloak, and her bleeding stopped at once. Jesus asked, 'Who touched me?'

Everyone denied it, and Peter said, 'Master, the people are all round you and crowding in on you.'

But Jesus said, 'Someone touched me, for I knew it when power went out of me.' The woman saw that she had been found out, so she came trembling and threw herself at Jesus' feet. There in front of everybody, she told him why she had touched him and how she had been healed at once. Jesus said to her, 'My daughter, your faith has made you well. Go in peace.'

Luke 8:42–48

The healing love of God

Jesus said, 'Let the children come to me, and do not stop them, because the Kingdom of heaven belongs to such as these.'

Matthew 19:14

The disciples had attempted to prevent the children being brought to Jesus but they misunderstood. Jesus reaches out to everyone. His love penetrates our deepest hurts and the two poems which follow, written by two prisoners, one at Holloway and the other at Lincoln, describe the closeness of God's love whenever we call out to him.

The Lord is with me

The Lord is with me, I know no fear
though I am in prison;
you let me free from my chains
you ask no price.
You do only what is right,
I fear no man now you are near
I believe in your words, now I am here
I have repented my sins,
I asked you Lord into my poor life
you show me the right path to take—
forgiven me my countless mistakes.
You have given me peace—
the strength to go on—
my life in your family
I hope will be long—
my trust and love in you Lord ever strong.
The Lord is with me
in him I am safe—
the Lord is with me
my poor soul he has saved.

K.H.

Thoughts of you

*Can it be true
what I now see
my eyes are old
are they deceiving me?*

*Within me now
my senses revive
my heart was dead
it's now alive.*

*Long have I looked
across the fields in tears
the long days and weeks
have grown into years.*

*My eyes so pained
and covered in dew
your beauty did astound me
when I first noticed you.*

*Love is everything
without the 'me'.
Love is all
when Jesus I see.*

*Every thought of you
is a thought of great price
individually, collectively
one feeling of 'nice'.*

*I may wish to explore
some thought anew
but there's nowhere I can go
to escape the thoughts of you.*

M.H.

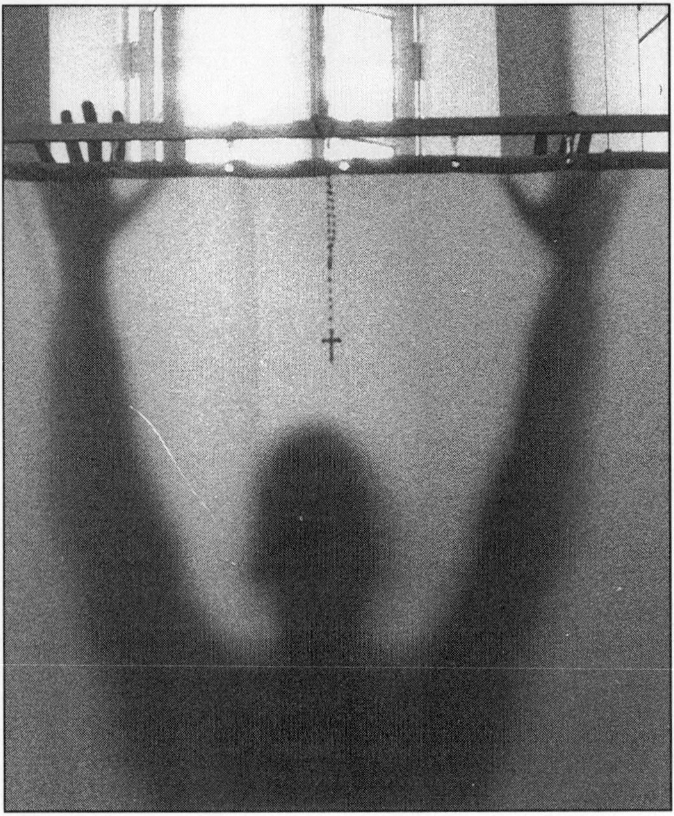

Knock back!

One of the most moving experiences in my life was sitting in a prison cell and praying with a prisoner for God to touch that man's heart. As we prayed that moment the room seemed to be filled with heat and the prisoner and I were moved to tears. I spoke some words aloud—I can't remember exactly what—but the prisoner—my brother in Christ—repeated them, asking Jesus to come into his life. For us both it was an unexpected and supernatural experience, as though through our tears, in the presence of the living God, the past was being restored and new life was being breathed in. This is no romantic account; it is what really happened. And, for this brother in Christ, new life is a day-to-day experience. He is serving a life sentence, so it is not always easy for him to accept his situation and I know there have been times when he has felt like giving up altogether, but he hasn't.

'Knock back' is his story.

Richard's story

When I was seventeen I was given a discretionary life sentence for GBH with intent to kill. I am now thirty years old and although my tariff was eight years, I have spent thirteen years inside. In 1993 I went up for parole for the third time and somehow I knew it was not going to be successful.

I haven't been an 'angel' since I have been in prison and after the first two knock backs all I wanted to do was fight the system. What I didn't realize was that it would seriously affect me later on. Getting knocked back really hurt.

Over the past two years I have started to search for God and although becoming a Christian in prison has not been easy for me, it has opened up a more peaceful life within myself. I know that it is because of the experience of Jesus in my life that I have been able to accept the third knock back. It's still hard and it still hurts but because of God I now have hope for a different future.

Crime doesn't pay; it hurts the victim, your family and you; but God is able, and wants, to give us all the chance to change ourselves and our situations. If we turn to him then we can see a new life of love and of hope.

God's promise to me

God's promise to all who put their trust in him is that he will be with them. God also requires of us that we love one another, and it is often in the ordinary act of kindness that the power of God is most evident.

The story of the Good Samaritan is a powerful illustration of how one person can make a dramatic difference to another. However, the story is also a reminder that when we try and help another person there is a limitation to what we are able to do, and that God is the luggage bearer. We do not need to become overburdened by others, only to reach out as far as we are able. The other side of this story is the view from the person needing help. Abandoned and neglected by those who had the power and the authority to help.

Jesus answered, 'There was once a man who was going down from Jerusalem to Jericho when robbers attacked him, stripped him, and beat him up, leaving him half dead. It so happened that a priest was going down that road; but when he saw the man, he walked on by, on the other side. In the same way a Levite also came along, went over and looked at the man, and then walked on by, on the other side. But a Samaritan who was travelling that way came upon the man, and when he saw him, his heart was filled with pity. He went over to him, poured oil and wine on his wounds and bandaged them; then he put the man on his own animal and took him to an inn, where he took care of him. The next day he took out two silver coins and gave them to the innkeeper. "Take care of him," he told the innkeeper, "and when I come back this way, I will pay you whatever else you spend on him."'

And Jesus concluded, 'In your opinion, which one of these three acted like a neighbour towards the man attacked by the robbers?'

The teacher of the Law answered, 'The one who was kind to him.' Jesus replied, 'You go, then, and do the same.'

Luke 10:30–37

Alan Duce is the chaplain at Lincoln prison and he explains how he sees his role as a Christian reaching out to those in need.

It's certainly true that prisoners can make remarks like, 'I feel shut off,' 'No one understands me,' 'I feel lost,' and when that's said to me I don't disagree with it. I'm not able to enter their mind-set but I want to help them to be able to talk more about where they see they are at the moment.

Everyone we meet is a very precious individual in God's eyes and if the specialness of the person is recognized, appreciated and responded to then it will come out in different ways.

In the Bible, God approaches people in different sorts of ways. When Jesus met people he handled them in individual ways. As representatives of the Church it is our task to meet people where they actually are.

In a prison you meet such human tragedy. I think it is difficult for a prisoner to anticipate that when they come to a prison they will meet someone like a Chaplain who will be useful to them, because they will come with such bitterness their expectations will not be very high.

I was very conscious when I was in hospital that people who lived very disadvantaged lives in London came into a hospital and suddenly received tremendous care by the doctors and nurses. They had to be sent back home but it was one of the times they realized that they could be cared for. It is a dream on my part that someone could come to prison and find that there was a surprisingly different emphasis in the Chaplaincy or other good staff that could astonish them.

I see prisoners who find it very hard to realize that God is a loving God. They may feel very oppressed, especially if there is an injustice in their being in prison. All I can be is a representative of God. It is not for me to speak God's words of judgment—it is for me to help people judge themselves and judge the circumstances that have engulfed them. Which is different from judging God. It's very easy to be angry with God when you have nobody else nearer at hand to be angry with.

I think I used to try to answer the question about anger towards God by being very rational about it. But at the end of the day you cannot be very rational about God. You have got to come to God on a level that is emotional and self-effacing and put yourself in God's hands to receive God's grace.

Prison is very self-absorbing and people can be very absorbed in their own problems. They don't want to see things in a wider light—which is what spiritual and theological understanding wants to encourage us towards. To put ourselves totally in God's hands, separate from the worldly things that are engulfing us, and put all our trust in God.

I never had a flash of light and I don't relate to St Paul's experience but there was one prisoner who was a former drug addict who I met at Fern prison. He was, to the world, a very disturbed person but most likeable, and he really believed that God spoke to people at the most dramatic moments.

One day he said to a prison officer, 'Kneel down with me and take the Lord into your heart.' The officer didn't kneel down, but afterwards he said to me that what the prisoner said was very important, 'and I know that I should have knelt down but as a prison officer I couldn't'. One should never underestimate the tremendous individuality there is in people. I am often amazed at prisoners who have been so downcast yet can find God within themselves—and the resources to come up again.

God's promise of help

I look to the mountains;
where will my help come from?
My help will come from the Lord,
who made heaven and earth.
He will not let you fall;
your protector is always awake.
The protector of Israel
never dozes or sleeps.
The Lord will guard you;
he is by your side to protect you.
The sun will not hurt you during the day,
nor the moon during the night.

The Lord will protect you from all danger;
he will keep you safe.
He will protect you as you come and go
now and for ever.

Psalm 121

The Psalmist writes about how God will protect us from falling and how he always watches over us. Sometimes I am asked why God has allowed certain things to happen. Nearly always when a particular situation is looked at closely we can see that what happened usually began with a choice. We have free will, an independent spirit, which does not necessarily help us to choose good things, or things which keep us from harm.

Forgiveness

Jason Richards found God, and found forgiveness, through searching and through reading the Bible. But it was really Jesus who found Jason. This is his story.

I was in Parkhurst Prison. I hadn't been long in my sentence and I was very confused. About myself and about life. I was carrying an awful lot of guilt. And I was looking for answers. I was trying to work out whether life had any meaning any more. Or whether I knew what meaning was.

I read a lot. I read Aleister Crowley. I read Buddhism. I read Islam. I started reading the Bible. And the more I read the Scriptures the more I became aware of God.

I didn't believe in God. I was actually an atheist—or at least I thought I was. But I came to believe that God existed. And the more I became aware of God the more I became aware that I was a sinner—and I got more and more desperate.

I knew I was alienated from God and that I was beyond the pale. I could see things as light and darkness. I could see the bad side of the world. And the light. I could see what was good. And I knew that I was on the wrong side—and I didn't want to be on that side any more.

I no longer wanted to identify with the corruption and the greed and the selfishness. I wanted to be on God's side. Yet it was as though I couldn't be. That drove me to a point of desperation. I thought at one stage, 'Well, if I really work hard, and I try and tell other people about God, then maybe at the end of the day he will say to me: You have made an effort, Jason... Maybe then he'll accept me at the last moment.'

But even though I was thinking that, I didn't believe it in my heart. I was saying to myself, 'You're finished. You're beyond the pale. There is no way that you can make up for what you've been and what you've done. It's impossible.'

Deep down there was this conflict. I could see—like two armies—a darkness and a light. I desperately wanted to change. But I couldn't. Then one night I was in my cell and I just let go totally. My sanity completely went and it was as though I was going into a black hole. Everything seemed to come to an end and there was nothing left.

Then I just cried out. I actually shouted: 'God, have mercy on me!' Then I opened the Bible and it opened up at the Psalms. At the very first Psalm. I started reading, and then I fell on my knees. And I started crying. I have never wept like that. It was like all of my life went before me. I didn't want to see it. I didn't want to look at it. All of the terrible things.

I just carried on reading—and when I got to Psalms 50 and 51 I realized that God would forgive me. Psalm 51 was King David's Psalm that he wrote after he had had Bathsheba, and had Bathsheba's husband Uriah the Hittite killed. I didn't know all that then. But the thing that I knew was 'Save me from bloodguilt, O God, the God who saves me, and my tongue will sing of your righteousness.'

That whole Psalm has become my life. Because as soon as I became a Christian I started singing and being involved with music. I'm always singing about God and about my experience of God. It's not something I planned. It's just happened over the years.

But I knew that God could forgive me. And I just said, 'OK. I don't care what it is. I'm yours. I'll do whatever you want. That's it. You'll have to teach me.' I didn't know anything about Jesus or the Bible or the Church. I just knew. I read all the rest of the Psalms on my knees—and almost from that point for me they became Psalms of praise. It was like I was beginning to worship—and I didn't know what worship was. I don't know what time I went to bed that night. But I woke up and the whole world was light...

Be merciful to me, O God,
because of your constant love.
Because of your great mercy
wipe away my sins!
Wash away all my evil
and make me clean from my sin!

I recognize my faults;
I am always conscious of my sins.
I have sinned against you—only against you—
and done what you consider evil.
So you are right in judging me;
you are justified in condemning me.
I have been evil from the day I was born;
from the time I was conceived,
I have been sinful.

Sincerity and truth are what you require;
fill my mind with your wisdom.
Remove my sin, and I will be clean;
wash me, and I will be whiter than snow.
Let me hear the sounds of joy and gladness;
and though you have crushed me and broken me,
I will be happy once again.
Close your eyes to my sins
and wipe out all my evil.

Create a pure heart in me, O God,
and put a new and loyal spirit in me.
Do not banish me from your presence;
do not take your holy spirit away from me.
Give me again the joy that comes from your
salvation,
and make me willing to obey you.
Then I will teach sinners your commands,
and they will turn back to you.

Spare my life, O God, and save me,
and I will gladly proclaim your righteousness.
Help me to speak, Lord,
and I will praise you.

You do not want sacrifices,
or I would offer them;
you are not pleased with burnt offerings.
My sacrifice is a humble spirit, O God;
you will not reject a humble and repentant heart.

Psalm 51:1–17

In the story of King David and Bathsheba, David chose to break one of God's commandments and this in turn led to several more being broken, ending up with murder. However, God loved David and because David was willing to turn away—Christians call this repenting—from the past and face God, fully accepting the actions he had chosen were wrong, God was able to forgive David and restore him.

Here Patrick tells his story and how, recognizing that he is responsible for his current situation, and being able to forgive the wrong that others have done to him, he is able to move on and accept God's promise of forgiveness.

Patrick's story

I've been in a few places for young offenders. The first time I got in trouble, my stepfather had lost his job. He started drinking and getting violent. He used to come home at night and take every bit of money so the only thing we could do, we were still at school, was steal. His mum had just died but I feel angry he was taking from us; he'd bought us up since we were kids. We needed him.

When I first came into this prison I met the Father of the Chapel and I talked about my life. I wasn't afraid to cry, but being in prison has made me think, 'What's it all about? Where did I go wrong?' I don't want to make the same mistake again but it's going to be hard. I want to get out and be straight but I can't do it on my own. When I get released next month I've got some help from probation and I've got a lot of support from my girlfriend, but if I come back to prison

I am going to lose her. Two of my best mates are doing life—I don't want to follow in their footsteps over one mistake.

Last year I got baptized in prison. I wanted to change. I wanted to believe in God. I sit on my bed at nighttime and I think: Thank you, God, for getting me through this day. I've learned to read and write in prison. I'm learning and God is helping me. I know he will speak to me one day. When I pray for my kids and for my family and for my friends, it takes a weight off my shoulders.

I've been in months and months. I have a mate who is getting out tomorrow. I still feel glad for him, but I feel down when I talk about getting out. Sometimes things are bound to go wrong—that is why I get depressed, because I don't want things to go wrong.

I have done something wrong—I am not with my children, not with my girl, but it is my own fault. After my last sentence I tried for a job. The interviewer asked if I had been to prison. I told him the truth, I didn't want to lie. I told him what I had done and why I had done it. Another guy got the job, although I had more qualifications than he did and I am good at drawing as a technician. I was really disappointed but I think it was the tattoos on my face—and prison.

When I was baptized in Warrington Prison, I felt special. I felt warm inside and I could tell the whole world about my problems. I felt like God had put his arms around me. I felt warm and I was very happy. To me Jesus is a father. I look on him as a father and he gets me through the day. I believe he is there all the time for me.

Jerry Stevens is a Chaplain at a prison in London. This is how he sees the need for us to forgive and be forgiven.

Forgiveness is something we all need. We all need to be assured that, no matter what we've done, the people we've wronged will forgive us. Of course one of the problems is that they need to know that we are truly sorry for the misery and the harm that we've caused them. One of the problems for men who are serving a life sentence for murder is very often that they come here isolated from their family. Or, because of the long time they are serving, marriages break down, because of the problem of holding the relationship together with so many barriers in between them.

I think the men are realistic enough to know that often they are not going to be able to hold on to their partners, and in some cases they actually even encourage their partner to make another life for themselves without them. Very often they can find forgiveness for people who really have let them down. The biggest problem is not being able to forgive themselves. Many of the men have murdered someone they loved and cared for. They find it very hard to accept that not only can people forgive them, but God can forgive them.

The men often find it difficult because they have had no real relationship with God. One of the problems is the idea of the father figure—to a lot of them, 'father' does not equal a good relationship. So by focusing their attention on the humanity of Jesus' death on the cross they can then relate to him as a human being. Hopefully we can then build on that relationship to refocus on the divinity of Christ.

There is nothing that God cannot forgive but it depends on the person asking for forgiveness. For forgiveness to be true there also needs to be true repentance.

> No, in all these things we have complete victory through him who loved us! For I am certain that nothing can separate us from his love: neither death nor life, neither angels nor other heavenly rulers or powers, neither the present nor the future, neither the world above nor the world below—there is nothing in all creation that will ever be able to separate us from the love of God which is ours through Christ Jesus our Lord.
>
> Romans 8:37–39

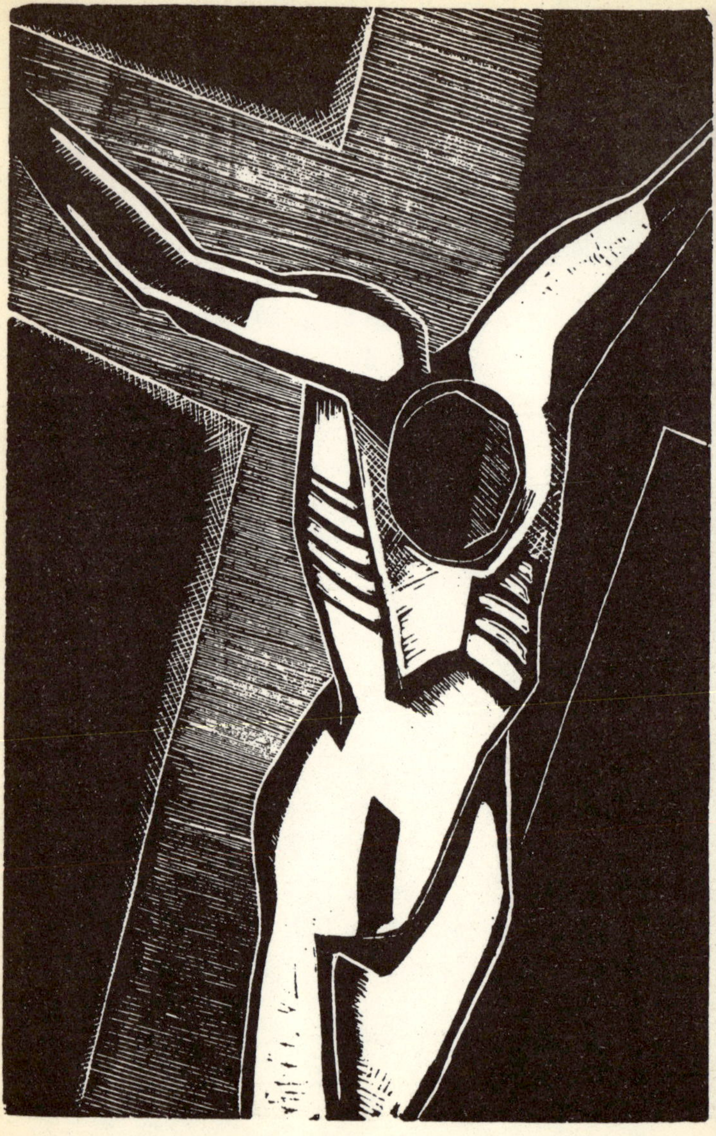

New life

Jesus said to one of the criminals being crucified alongside him that he (the criminal) would be in paradise with Jesus. When we turn towards the cross and accept God we are at the beginning of a new life. There are three steps to achieving this beginning. First, we must be willing to accept that we have not lived according to God's word; secondly, we must wish to turn away from that past way of life and ask for forgiveness; and thirdly we must ask Jesus to come into our hearts and live in us. There is no one person for whom this is not true, but there are many who do not take this step of faith—as with the man crucified on the other side of Jesus.

The soldiers led Jesus away, and as they were going, they met a man from Cyrene named Simon who was coming into the city from the country. They seized him, put the cross on him, and made him carry it behind Jesus.

A large crowd of people followed him; among them were some women who were weeping and wailing for him. Jesus turned to them and said, 'Women of Jerusalem! Don't cry for me, but for yourselves and your children. For the days are coming when people will say, "How lucky are the women who never had children, who never bore babies, who never nursed them!" That will be the time when people will say to the mountains, "Fall on us!" and to the hills, "Hide us!" For if such things as these are done when the wood is green, what will happen when it is dry?'

Two other men, both of them criminals, were also led out to be put to death with Jesus. When they came to the place called 'The Skull', they crucified Jesus there, and the two criminals, one on his right and the other on his left. Jesus said, 'Forgive them, Father! They don't know what they are doing.'

They divided his clothes among themselves by throwing dice. The people stood there watching while the Jewish leaders jeered at him: 'He saved others; let him save himself if he is the Messiah whom God has chosen!'

The soldiers also mocked him: they came up to him and offered him cheap wine, and said, 'Save yourself if you are the king of the Jews!'

Above him were written these words: 'This is the King of the Jews.'

One of the criminals hanging there hurled insults at him: 'Aren't you the Messiah? Save yourself and us!'

The other one, however, rebuked him, saying, 'Don't you fear God? You received the same sentence he did. Ours, however, is only right, because we are getting what we deserve for what we did; but he has done no wrong.' And he said to Jesus, 'Remember me, Jesus, when you come as King!'

Jesus said to him, 'I promise you that today you will be in Paradise with me.'

Luke 23:26–43

Arthur Mann is on the Chaplaincy team at Lincoln Prison. This is one story of his experience with a prisoner who sought new life.

I don't think many people outside prison life understand the trauma that prisoners are in. Prisoners are not vile people, although what they have done is vile. God loves the sinner but hates the sin. If we truly believe the word of God, when he died on the cross, Jesus destroyed even the deepest work of the devil. The worst person on earth can come to salvation. The Scripture quite clearly says whoever the Son (Jesus) sets free is free indeed. It's a fact that a great percentage of prisoners do reoffend, but I believe if a person truly repents for his crime he will find forgiveness and freedom.

We had a young man here who was a Liverpudlian. A redhead. You put the two together and you've got fire! He had a traumatic time because of his lifestyle, and he was violent. He got put in prison and this time his wife said that's it. They had four or five children. I began to talk to him and he got a week's home leave. Through prayer and talking together everything was settled with his wife. God entered that man's life and changed him completely.

In this story, Jesus has his feet washed by Mary. The rulers of the town considered Mary a 'sinful woman'. They judged her and they also judged Jesus because he allowed the woman to touch him. Jesus in turn tells another story and challenges the judgment of the rulers. This story is also a challenge for us today.

Jesus anointed by a sinful woman

A Pharisee invited Jesus to have dinner with him, and Jesus went to his house and sat down to eat. In that town was a woman who lived a sinful life. She heard that Jesus was eating in the Pharisee's house, so she brought an alabaster jar full of perfume and stood behind Jesus, by his feet, crying and wetting his feet with her tears. Then she dried his feet with her hair, kissed them, and poured the perfume on them. When the Pharisee saw this, he said to himself, 'If this man really were a prophet, he would know who this woman is who is touching him; he would know what kind of sinful life she lives!'

Jesus spoke up and said to him, 'Simon, I have something to tell you.'

'Yes, Teacher,' he said, 'tell me.'

'There were two men who owed money to a moneylender,' Jesus began. 'One owed him five hundred silver coins, and the other owed him fifty. Neither of them could pay him back, so he cancelled the debts of both. Which one, then, will love him more?'

'I suppose,' answered Simon, 'that it would be the one who was forgiven more.'

'You are right,' said Jesus. Then he turned to the woman and said to Simon, 'Do you see this woman? I came into your home, and you gave me no water for my feet, but she has washed my feet with her tears and dried them with her hair. You did not welcome me with a kiss, but she has not stopped kissing my feet since I came. You provided no olive oil for my head, but she has covered my feet with perfume. I tell you, then, the great love she has shown proves that her many sins have been forgiven. But whoever has been forgiven little shows only a little love.'

Then Jesus said to the woman, 'Your sins are forgiven.'

The others sitting at the table began to say to themselves, 'Who is this, who even forgives sins?'

But Jesus said to the woman, 'Your faith has saved you; go in peace.'

Luke 7:36–50

It is so easy for us to judge each other but God promises new life through forgiveness. Danny has experienced exactly that. This is his story.

Danny's story

Prison didn't feel like life at all to me. From the start I felt that I'd failed. There was no hope—I was written off. When you have been arrested you're sitting in the police station and you cannot believe it's happened to you. Everything is taken from you: your job, your whole life, your family breaking down. I never had any hope at all.

After I had been inside for about a year I applied for and got the Chaplaincy 'red band' job. Before then the only contact I had with other people was on visits with family and friends; the rest of the time I was with officers and inmates.

I began to feel different—part of life on the outside again. The conversation was not bars- or prison-orientated. I realized that I could do something and I was able to accept my sentence. I wasn't treated with suspicion and that helped me relax. I got coffee once a week, real coffee with sugar. I had the freedom of walking around, and the trust.

Once I got the trust I felt better in myself. Once I relaxed I was able to receive God. I would be fooling myself if I said it was the relaxed atmosphere which brought me to reality. Trust is the main thing—trust.

No matter where I go now people say 'he's an ex-con' but I know I am forgiven by Jesus. If my next-door neighbour doesn't forgive me, that is his problem. As long as I have forgiveness from God that is the only thing I worry about. If you get yourself into difficult situations, which everybody does, the only way to get through is to accept who you are and come to terms with what you have done. Once you are able to do that, with Christ you can be free even inside prison.

If you do not come to terms with yourself and carry on the problems you will always be carrying them. You accept that as a reason why you commit more crime but it is an excuse. If you have faith to believe that you are forgiven you can go out there with confidence and you will be surprised how far you can reach with that faith.

It is the way forward but you can only get that total forgiveness through God, you can't get it from people. Someone asked me how long I have been out. I said since 1993. He said, 'Last year,' and I said, 'Yeah, last year, only last year.' I have gone a long way.

Mike is an instructor in a prison tailor's shop. He has worked in the prison for five years and recognizes that living a Christian life in prison is not always easy—but then, neither is living as a Christian in a secular world.

We are creatures of feeling—often we don't feel like praying or praising God. At these times the enemy is very subtle and will try to steal away our faith.

God will refine us and mature us
God is for us and not against us

Being a Christian in prison I can be misunderstood, regarded as a goody—I believe in justice, I'm not a softy. God can forgive but we reap what we sow. We are judged by God's plumb-line and his judgment is fair and righteous—our actions do have repercussions.

God said to the children of Israel: you can choose life or you can choose death. Forgiving ourselves is hard—and we must forgive those who have sinned against us. God cannot forgive us otherwise.

Like the spider who weaves a silk web and hopes to attract food we can often be attracted to shimmering glittery things. Or we will try to get our mess straight, only to fall back into the same old trap. By expressing ourselves creatively, we too can acknowledge what really needs to happen for change to take place and new life to begin.

New life can find us in many different ways—often when we express ourselves in creativity. We begin to be open to the new life of God—the Creator of all.

I was visiting Dartmoor Prison and my tour of the prison, for no particular reason, ended in the gym. The Dartmoor gym is like any other, except that on the walls are some striking murals of men in various athletic attitudes, weight-lifting, vaulting and so on. The officer told me the story behind them. Some years before they had a difficult inmate. He even called himself 'John Rebel'. Someone realized he'd been a signwriter before conviction and they got him to decorate the gym with the murals I saw. The interesting thing is that the first ones he did, he simply signed 'JR', the later ones, 'John Rebel'. And the ones he painted last, he signed with his own real name.

John Rebel found himself—acknowledged who he was—through his own creative activity. That is often the way God works in us. And we need to help each other to enable that to happen...

If the Spirit of God, who raised Jesus from death, lives in you, then he who raised Christ from death will also give life to your mortal bodies by the presence of his Spirit in you.

Romans 8:11

+ *Robert Lincoln*

*I wait eagerly for the Lord's help,
and in his word I trust.*

Psalm 130:5

Unconditional love

In the Book of Isaiah, God speaks through the prophet and, even though the people of Israel have broken God's law and all their promises, he speaks to them of his forgiveness through love.

So often the words 'I love you' accompany some other hidden meaning and we can abuse the very essence of love which is found in truth and respect. God's love for us is pure. He does not make it conditional on our past behaviour, what we look like, on where we live, or how much money we have. He longs for us to receive his unconditional love.

'When my people in their need look for water,
when their throats are dry with thirst,
then I, the Lord, will answer their prayer;
I, the God of Israel, will never abandon them.
I will make rivers flow among barren hills
and springs of water run in the valleys.
I will turn the desert into pools of water
and the dry land into flowing springs.
I will make cedars grow in the desert,
and acacias and myrtles and olive trees.
Forests will grow in barren land,
forests of pine and juniper and cypress.
People will see this and know
that I, the Lord, have done it.
They will come to understand
that Israel's holy God has made it happen.

Isaiah 41:17–20

God's promise of unconditional love

*God is in prison with me
God is in the darkness with me
God is in the confusion with me
God is in my hopelessness*

*His hands hold mine—
I reach out, touch him, nearby
smell the sweetness of his presence.*

God is. 'I am', and therefore so am I in him.

Liza Davies

When I can't go on

Anne is one of the Chaplaincy team at HMP Belmarsh. Like many other prison staff she often meets men who have come to the end of the road. Whose burdens are so heavy they can't carry on.

I remember one young prisoner in his twenties. I did a lot of work in the health care centre and one day when I was there the officers asked me to speak to this young guy. He had reached rock bottom. He was suicidal and he was pretty desperate because of his family circumstances. I visited him often after that and I noticed he gradually began to improve. I think if he had the means he would have killed himself.

A few months later I was driving along in the car and at the traffic light a guy got out and said, 'Do you remember me?' It was him and he was just so totally different, I was terribly encouraged to see someone so despairing so improved. I've got no doubt that the spiritual approach had helped him, that his hope was restored.

Isaiah 43:1–7 promises that whatever we are like, we are precious to the Lord. When we pass through the waters he will be with us.

*Israel, the Lord who created you says,
'Do not be afraid—I will save you.
I have called you by name—you are mine.
When you pass through deep waters,
I will be with you;
your troubles will not overwhelm you.
When you pass through fire, you will not be burnt;
the hard trials that come will not hurt you.
For I am the Lord your God,
the holy God of Israel, who saves you.
I will give up Egypt to set you free;
I will give up Ethiopia and Seba.
I will give up whole nations to save your life,
because you are precious to me
and because I love you and give you honour.
Do not be afraid—I am with you!*

*'From the distant east and the farthest west,
I will bring your people home.
I will tell the north to let them go
and the south not to hold them back.
Let my people return from distant lands,
from every part of the world.
They are my own people,
and I created them to bring me glory.'*

Isaiah 43:1–7

Brian's story

Brian became a Christian in 1980 but the relationship with his wife fell apart. After they divorced in 1989 he recommitted his life to God but three weeks later he was arrested and sent to prison for eight years. He too experienced such turmoil that life just didn't seem worth living anymore.

I had not expected to be arrested. I was scared—an indescribable fear of what was happening in an alien environment. On the first day I cried out to God with very deep prayers. One night, reading through the First Letter to the Corinthians, I asked to receive the Holy Spirit, and a few weeks later my prison visitor came to see me unexpectedly. He said he wanted to lay hands on me. I had been actively involved in some occult activities which I repented. At the same time I was so ashamed of my offence I couldn't admit to Mike, my visitor, what I had done, but as he prayed over me I experienced a warmth and prickling sensation in my chest.

If I hadn't been a Christian I probably would be dead—I attempted suicide on four different occasions. Prison has been a training ground for me, learning how to walk as a Christian and developing spiritual awareness.

I was only able to admit to Mike my guilt and crime six months ago. The hurt is still there and I still struggle but being able to admit my guilt has set me free.

Come Holy Spirit

*From the depths of my despair
I call to you, Lord.
Hear my cry, O Lord;
listen to my call for help!*

Psalm 130:1–2

The Holy Spirit is our comforter sent from God to help and heal us. After Jesus was baptized by John God sent the Holy Spirit to descend on Jesus in the form of a dove.

After all the people had been baptized, Jesus also was baptized. While he was praying, heaven was opened, and the Holy Spirit came down upon him in bodily form like a dove. And a voice came from heaven, 'You are my own dear Son. I am pleased with you.'

Luke 3:21–22

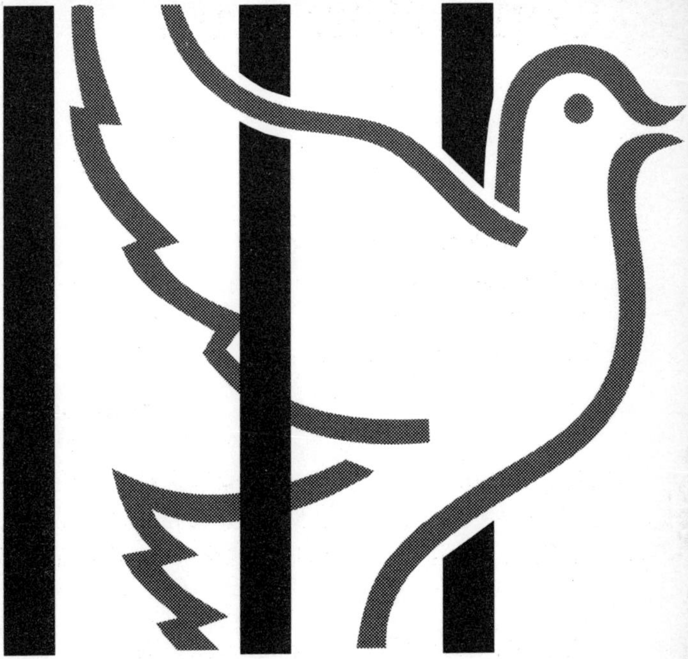

No way out

Colin is a Prison Governor. So often the relationships between prisoners and staff are strained and difficult, because of the nature of a system where one human being is deemed to have power over the freedom of another. However, many staff, officers, Governors and probation officers are concerned for men and women in custody. If we allow our humanity to overrule the badge of office, either as a member of staff or as a prisoner, we can create a relationship based on mutual trust and respect. Jesus asks us to keep the commandments, to love our neighbour as ourselves—whoever that neighbour be, and that includes prisoners and prison staff alike.

There was a particular bloke called W. in a closed prison where I was Governor. He was serving a second life sentence. The offences that he committed were so awful, I cannot remember exactly how long his sentence was. His marriage had broken up and he had lost contact with his child. The only person that really sustained him from outside was his mother and he used to get bouts of the blackest despair I've ever met in anybody.

At those times he couldn't handle normal prison life. He used to ask to go to the segregation unit in his black periods. On this occasion he was down there for months. It is very difficult to get lifers transferred, so not only was he was stuck in the system, he was stuck in a room in the segregation unit because he did not want to go anywhere else. I used to go to the segregation unit most days to see him and spend some time with him. We developed a relationship and I used to look forward to seeing him. When he got more and more remote I reached a stage with him, whether consciously or unconsciously, where the only thing I could say to him when I saw him and he refused to talk was, 'Good morning,' and, 'God bless you.' He did not want to speak.

The next part of the story is that he went through a great crisis when he tried to kill himself. He was only saved by the excellent work of night patrol. Later, one of the things that interested him and that he wrote in a letter to me was the fact that I'd said to him, 'God bless you.' I am not sure if I said it with deliberateness or whether it was my own kind of despair at not being able to help. The effect on him was tangible. In the way he noted it and responded to it I could feel something. I felt myself to be committing him to the safety of God because there was not any other mechanism to help him.

I think that is what is important to people in prison who are in a state of mind where they cannot be helped. That God does help in a very real quiet way.

The other thing I would say, which also relates to W., is some of the best people I have ever met in my life are prisoners. The reason I say that is because it is extremely difficult if you are incarcerated to hold a sense of good and bad and then have the courage to do something about it.

God has a plan for my life

One of the reasons I have often heard people give for not turning to God is that they are afraid he will 'change things'. Or, that the person feels that he or she needs to 'change things' before God will find them acceptable. In the Book of Revelation the following promise is given:

'Listen! I stand at the door and knock; if anyone hears my voice and opens the door, I will come in and eat with them, and they will eat with me.'

Revelation 3:20

Where Jesus lived eating together was a very important part of social activity. Unlike today when meals are often instant and hurried, dining together was taken over a long leisurely time during the afternoon and evening. By using this to illustrate his desire to enter into each of our hearts, God is demonstrating that he wants a relationship which will evolve and develop. He does not barge in, uninvited and turn us upside-down but rather enters, with grace, establishing his love at the very heart of our selves, however sad or damaged that heart might be. Malcolm's story is all about plans being changed by the presence of a loving God.

I suppose that if you'd said ten years ago I would be working in prison I would have fallen over laughing. Since I've been here everything I thought about people going into prison has been turned on its head. There is very little difference from those on the outside and inside. A few years ago, I was not a particularly nice guy. I first went to church when my secretary died and there I found this man Jesus. I had led a pretty wild life, probably a short step from being in prison myself. Since working here I have met men imprisoned for acts of violence, fighting and hurting somebody, and looking back on it I see some of me in some of them. I'm just thankful I didn't get put inside. I was into alcohol—an addict. I stopped drinking on one prayer. I had shouted at God: 'Are you going to stop me doing this?' I was drunk, but I have not touched a drop of Scotch since that time! People who knew me then are amazed.

I think what I hear most from the men here is, 'I am not good enough to be a Christian, I am a horrible bloke and I have got to tidy up all my problems first.' Something I have to disabuse them of is that you may not be ready to accept Jesus into your life but he is ready for you and he is ready to take anyone as they are. That doesn't mean you are going to be the world's best guy tomorrow but it is part of the process. Once you say yes, the rest is up to him! To some extent it's also you, but there is a change built into the acceptance that Jesus initiates and takes over. He will start to change you but you have to be prepared to join in the partnership, as it were—you have to listen. Don't think that what you feel in your heart is silly. It's not silly, it's real. I still need help with difficulties—they come up in any Christian's life. But help is there.

Danny is a very close friend of mine. During his sentence he was very depressed and his wife had left him. We have a small group on Wednesdays so I said let's get the guys here to pray for you. One night I went out on the landing and he came running down with a letter in his hand and some photographs. The letter said, 'Dear Danny, we can still be friends and I will come to see you.' He said, 'It's worked hasn't it, the praying has worked.' His wife said that he could stay at her new flat on his home leave quite close to prison. They established a new relationship. When he was due to go out he was very nervous and one day he came to me and showed me a letter from his wife. 'Dear Danny, I don't know how to tell you this but while you have been in prison I have become a born-again Christian, so when you come out we have changes to cope with.' Danny had been terrified to tell his wife about his own faith but now his commitment was complete.

During his last couple of months here he was a better witness than any of the Chaplaincy team. Danny and his wife worked together to get the relationship going again. It was difficult at first because it was a new type of relationship. Danny's now been tutored to preach and he gets invited to churches all over England to talk about his experiences. His story is so powerful.

In Matthew 25 Jesus said that we will be judged not by what we say but how we express our love to others. I think it's something every Christian should read at least once a week.

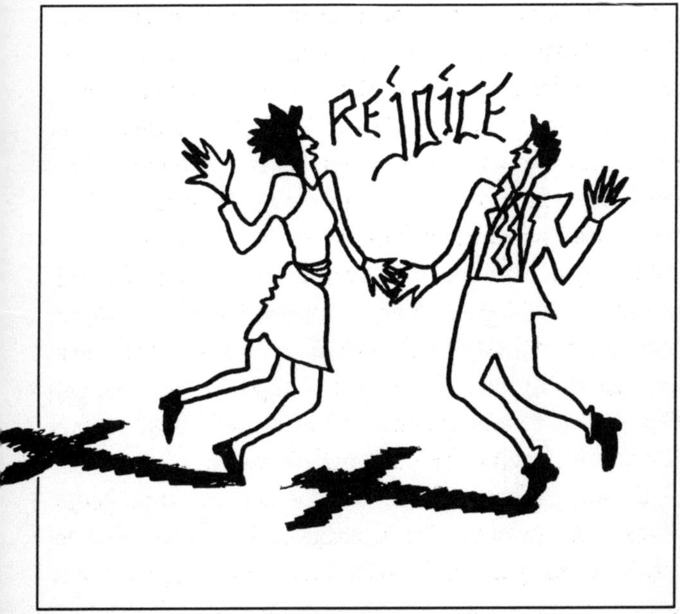
REJOICE

What's the purpose of my life?

What's the purpose of my life?
I live alone,
maybe to run a family home,
to be a wife!
What am I meant to do with life?
Do I follow my childhood dreams?
Will they be all that they once seemed?
I need someone to show me the way,
lonely in life I don't want to stay.
Life has a purpose,
a meaning—just
Lord in your guidance I shall trust.

K.H.

This verse was given to me from the Lord by his Holy Spirit on my way home one evening from a social club only a short walk from my house. I have never before or since written a poem or verse and although I am in prison my faith has not been shattered, for *in him I will abide*.

> *I walk with the Lord*
> *and He takes my hand*
> *for He is by my side*
> *He leads me on*
> *to greater things and*
> *in Him I will abide.*

R.S.

The still small voice

*The unseen God all knowing yet silent
and speaking into my silence.*

*The invisible God yet visible to me
and ever present in my despair.*

*The peaceful God who gives me power
and invites me to share the power of his peace.*

*The loving God who created me
and in whose love I can trust forever.*

Liza Davies

Colin has worked as an art teacher in the prison service for many years. He is a professional artist and uses his gifts to help men in prison develop their own gifts and talents—often, for them, for the first time. As a Christian, Colin recognizes that within a prison our emotions can penetrate very deeply.

A prison cell can be a place of confinement and punishment, a place where feelings of self-pity, anger, revenge, loneliness and desolation swirl in turbulent confusion. God is within us but we often do not realize this. He lives within us as the Holy Spirit and one way he speaks to us is through our moods and feelings. To hear him speak we need to learn how to relax and be still. To accept honestly how we feel and to be prepared to face the truth about ourselves. In the silence and the stillness he will make himself known to us.

I think God is much closer than we realize—our problem is that we don't recognize him in the ordinary and we don't see him there. Part of the spiritual pilgrimage is being able to become sensitive to God in the ordinary things—a genuine awareness of his presence.

It's a question of belief in God in our darkness—as Gerard Hughes said, the facts are kind (God is in the facts) although we don't always perceive that as such. I am not dependent on the role I play in this place. My identity is in who I am, who God made me to be. It's felt very much like our childhood ideas of God fall away and we have to find a new understanding. Like walking down a dark road at night—the darkness continues and we get used to it. The darkness doesn't need to be negative or heavy—the old ideas fall away and new rules come into play which give us more choice.

There are still hazards but there is a greater freedom—being alive to God's presence in the ordinariness, through the choices I make. My feelings of anger, bitterness and so on can thwart the ultimate that I am able to create, because we don't see God as big enough to take us as we are on his shoulders—the journey of discovery of our inner selves.

The peace of God

Can a bustling busy prison ever be a place of peace? Perhaps not. But inwardly if we are at peace with ourselves, with others and with God then that peace can transcend the noise and disruption of our surroundings.

In his letter to the church at Philippi, St Paul prayed that they would receive God's peace which passes all understanding. This prayer is echoed in The Book of Common Prayer, from which the prayer below is taken.

My prayer for you today is that you too will find that peace.

The peace of God, which passeth all understanding, keep your hearts and minds in the knowledge and love of God, and of his Son Jesus Christ our Lord: and the blessing of God Almighty, the Father, the Son, and the Holy Ghost, be amongst you and remain with you always.

Lakeside

A lonely figure
By the lake
Reaching out
As the waters break

Just a ripple
A minor deflection
Awesome beauty
In the sun's reflection

Words cannot express
The peaceful scene
The lonely figure
Goes unseen

No suggestion
Of slipping or sliding
Upon the water
Gently gliding

A beautiful presence
To Thee adore
Those tired feet
Reach the shore

A total serenity
Enriches my eyes
My heart and mind
In paradise

M.H.